The Prophetic Staff

Ken Cox

Copyright © 2017 by Ken Cox

All rights reserved
Rejoice Essential Publishing
P.O. BOX 512
Effingham, SC 29541
www.republishing.org

All rights reserved. No part of this book may be used or reproduced by any means, graphic, electronic, or mechanical, including photocopying, recording, taping or by any information storage retrieval system without the written permission of the publisher except in the case of brief quotations embodied in critical articles and reviews.

Unless otherwise indicated, Scripture is taken from the King James Version.

Scriptures taken from the Holy Bible, New International Version®, NIV®. Copyright © 1973, 1978, 1984, 2011 by Biblica, Inc.™ Used by permission of Zondervan. All rights reserved worldwide. www.zondervan.com™

Visit the author's website at www.whereeaglesfly.us

The Prophetic Staff/ Ken Cox

ISBN-10: 1-946756-18-0
ISBN-13: 978-1-946756-18-3

Library of Congress Control Number: 2018931538

DEDICATION

My very special thanks to my wife, Prophetess Sabina Cox, who has stuck with me through thick and thin and showed me love, understanding, and most of all a necessary prophetic trait called patience. She is the reason I'm where I am today as she constantly educated and worked with me on acceptable standards of myself and those to whom God assigned to Where Eagles Fly Fellowship and Ministries, Inc. She has been and is my non-public prophetic voice and seer. To our Children, CJ, Arlina, and Kenneth Cox Jr. (AKA The Nature Boy) to their spouses and our Grandchildren, I say a heartfelt I love and thank you. I have been gone, and away at times on the battlefield for God and missed key events in your lives and I must say each one of you have been in my thoughts and prayers and I'm forever grateful to each of you for that, I humbly say thank you so much.

Welcome to the ministry of the prophetic staff. I also dedicate this book to you the reader, who I believe to be a prophet or interested in the prophetic ministry. Prophet, it is my prayer that you will grow, walk closer with God and that you will be benefitted as you walk in the ministry of the prophetic staff. We are servants, and this is a great tool that is so important to our lives as prophets. Welcome to the ministry of the prophetic staff. This book is dedicated to you prophet!

Table of Contents

Acknowledgements...viii
Preface..x
The Prophets Staff or Rod, which one?...............................1
Thy Rod and Thy Staff..9
A Piece of Wood..21
Positions of The Staff...28
The Prophet of Today and The Staff................................38
How do I find my Prophetic Staff.....................................46
Who can carry your Staff...57
A Closing Thought..64

ACKNOWLEDGEMENTS

The longer I live, the more thankful I am for the lessons of life. I dedicate this book to all those prophets before me who taught some of these same lessons and were never able to have them published. I salute all my spiritual and prophetic mentors who taught me many valuable lessons, like The Prophetic Staff Ministry that today seem to have been forgotten.

Preface

The prophetic staff represents the best of God as he proves to his prophets, the special relationship they only have with him. The prophetic staff, while not widely taught or used is and can be a vital part of any prophetic ministry. Some may say old school, others may look at it as a lost art, but this prophet sees God's miracle-working powers in the staff/rod of God.

The ministry of the prophetic staff has taken me years to understand, and even now, I'm still growing in this supernatural gift. As you read this book, my prayer is that you will understand how highly personal The Prophetic Staff ministry is. Make it your business to strive and learn more and more as you walk closer with God. This book will echo a common theme of how precious it is to walk with God and be available for his purposes.

Moses and other prophets who used the prophetic staff were walking close with God. I'm firmly under the belief that our mantles and relationships with God are proven as prophets by his works through us. The prophetic staff is a divine tool of God, to be used by a select group of elite prophets for his purposes. Understand that not every prophet will utilize the prophetic staff ministry.

My prophetic friend, as you read this, please do not make the following mistake that prophets make. You feel that you have been called to participate in the prophetic staff ministry, but you never realized the amount of suffering and preparation required on a personal level. When the process starts, running away, avoidance, or just to flat ignore and forget are all relevant options.

This is how this ministry gift is buried and quickly forgotten. The simple thing is that when you're not willing to walk through the process to be relevant in this gift, the blessings of this level intimacy with God are lost upon us. The intimacy is needed because you then graduate to fully passing, the leaders and people test who will struggle at best to understand your prophetic staff ministry. As you can see, it will be one test after another.

CHAPTER ONE

Introduction To The Prophets Staff

ROD VERSUS. STAFF

Many Hebrew terms are used to represent the words staff or rod. They are really one and the same, the difference is just how they are to be used, and by who they are to be used. Rod or Staff translate literally as, "a part," hence, branch, bar. We see this in the book of Exodus 25:13,14,15,27,28. There are other words like matteh[1], maqqel[2], shebhet[3], used also. They describe the staff in the hand, the shepherd's staff, figuratively, "staff of bread" Ezekiel 4:16; 5:16; 14:13, show us the Rod as indispensable for support of life. Let's also look at Matthew 10:10, Luke 9:3 and Hebrews 11:21. The New Testament word is rhabdos[4]. Many meanings of the terms staff and rod mean basically the same thing, except the cultures are different.

This is one of those important, but not discussed or spoken of nearly enough subjects. This is a prophetic issue that seem to fall through the cracks of our development. There simply is not enough exposure to The Prophetic Staff ministry. I often wonder today why we as prophets don't know more of this subject or practice the Prophetic Staff ministry more today. There's also a huge degree of confusion and misinformation in the prophetic ministry today as it is. Let's not dwell on that, let's look at the rod or staff. This will be important to your ministry if it is not already. Therefore, your reading this book now.

Webster's Revised Unabridged Dictionary[5] defines staff in the following ways:
1) As a long piece of wood; a stick; the long handle of an instrument or weapon; a pole or stick, used for many purposes; as a surveyor's staff; the staff of a spear or pike.
2) The Staff could be a stick carried in the hand for support or defense by a person walking; hence, support; that which props or upholds.
3) The staff is a pole, stick, or wand borne as an ensign of authority; a badge of office; as a constable's staff.

See there are many uses that we just don't seem to recognize today. The staff used by Moses, also called "rod" and Rod of God was always with him throughout every important milestone in his life. Prophets today, we see and then we don't see what does God give us to be with us in the most important events of our life. Since God changes not, are we to assume that he does not give us staffs today accomplish our missions? We see in Moses life, that the staff that was used to produce water from a rock, was transformed into a snake and back, and was used at the parting of the Red Sea. That's quite a bit. Does it make you wonder why, this is seemly a lost prophetic practice?

Prophets, now let's look at Exodus 4:2, the first introduction of the prophetic Staff to many of us. Moses acknowledges the staff in his hand and sees it transformed into a snake and then back into a staff. This would have scared many if not all of us. Depending on the translation and the prophet's situation the staff is referred to as the "rod of God" or "staff of God".

There are more supernatural examples of the rod or staff of God at work. Moses and Aaron as they appear before the pharaoh when Aaron's rod is transformed into a serpent and eats pharaoh's sorcerer's rods, which had been turned into serpents. This is the same rod that turns the Nile blood-red. The supernatural power of God is clearly at work, and you can't forget this prophet.

The work of the staff is seen with Moses as he stretches out his hand, with the staff to part the Red Sea. as he has led the people of God out of the wilderness. Moses also follows God's command to strike a rock with the rod or staff. This was to create a spring for all the Israelites to drink. This was also the insight on the sensitive nature of the prophetic staff ministry as we saw Moses strike the rock twice with his staff (Numbers 20:12). God punished the great Moses by not letting him enter the Promised Land.

Who can forget the classic battle at Rephidim between the Israelites and the Amalekites. Moses holds up the "rod of God" the Israelites "prevail", when he drops it because he is tired, their enemies gain the upper hand. Aaron and Hur help him to keep the staff raised until victory is achieved. They stood on each side of Moses.

Although the staff is frequently mentioned in the Word of God, it is surprising that scarcely anyone, especially prophets, seem to pay it much attention these days. What we see in the natural world is represented by spiritual world. Moses, we see that whenever he was commanded by God for a supernatural occurrence task always lifted his staff. The position of miracles and we will discuss this later.

This is a critical point, for those who want to move into supernatural ministry. We should not forget it as prophets. Do you realize the mentality and the level of faith he walked in? This is a gift to be sought after from God, no doubt. We, as prophets, will be made painfully aware of this in our efforts to go to this level. Welcome to the Process of understanding The Prophetic Staff ministry.

A staff, my staff or your staff prophet will be one that signifies power, because it is a support; for it supports the hand and arm, and through them the whole body; wherefore a staff takes on the signification of the part which it immediately supports, that is, the hand and arm of a prophet., by both of which in the Word of God is signified the power of truth.

In the life of a prophet, the staff was represented from what is related of Moses or any other prophet. Just as Moses was commanded to take his staff or rod, with which he was to do miracles, we are as well. The specifics of the Rod or Staff are in the 23rd Psalm in the same verse David had assurance that His Shepherd would lead him out of the valley. Jack Wellman states the shepherd never promised to take him over the valley, around the valley, or to avoid the valley but He did promise to go with him through the valley. That's why he was able to write that he would fear no evil, Psalm 23:4.

Briefly now prophet, understand the mentality of this anointing. Prophets that's the assurance we must have. He didn't say that he could avoid the evil, but he didn't have to fear the evil because the Great Shepherd would go with him in his encounters with evil, that's of special relief to the prophet. So, Prophet, why did the psalmist have no fear? It was because of his rod and His staff with Him. For this reason, there was no need to fear but why does the shepherd need both a rod and a staff? That's a really good question, let's get some answers.

Look at this, we see that rods were sometimes used as weapons of defense or offense and sometimes simply as a walking stick. A few times the rod and the staff were referred to as the same thing since the Hebrew word for rod is shebet, means both a rod or a staff but it can also mean "a club" as well (Gen 32:10). I told you there are multiple words that you can use to describe the Rod or Staff.

Prophets, understand this, most of the time the rod was a symbol of correction and discipline like when Solomon wrote Proverbs 13:24. It states, "Whoever spares the rod hates his son, but he who loves him is diligent to discipline him." The covenant that God made with David the Lord said of Solomon, "I will be to him a father, and he shall be to me a son" (2nd Sam 7:14).

When he commits iniquity, I will discipline him with the rod of men, with the stripes of the sons of men. God does not mean that He would beat Solomon with an actual rod but God was using this word as an expression of His discipline of Solomon when he would need it and like us he surely would need to.

This is a sign of love because love equals discipline and the opposite of love is indifference. Hebrews 12:6 says "The Lord disciplines the one he loves and chastises every son whom he receives." Psalm 94:12 says "Blessed is the one you discipline, LORD, the one you teach from your law". Psalm 119:75 says, "In faithfulness you have afflicted me." For we know that surely the LORD disciplines those he loves.

Today in many parts of the world, We still see shepherds carry rods and staffs to protect and care for their sheep but the staff has a significantly different meaning and use than the rod. The staff is symbolic of God's authority as His leaders (Exodus 7-10). We see Moses' staff and how it was involved with the plagues given out to Egypt that indicated God's sovereignty over Egypt.

In Isaiah 15:5, we see that the staff was also a referred to as a sign of a ruler like a king's scepter. Isaiah wrote "The Lord has broken the staff of the wicked, the scepter of rulers" and of a nation when God referred to Egypt as "that broken reed of a staff (Isaiah 36:6)." The prophet Micah referred to the staff, writing "Shepherd your people with your staff, the flock of your inheritance, who dwell alone in a forest in the midst of a garden land (Micah 7:14)".

So now let's look at this fact prophet, God loves us so much not to leave us to ourselves. He cares enough to discipline us with His metaphorical rod when we need it. If He didn't love us, He'd let us wander off like sheep over a cliff. His rod protects us from the enemy and He will use His staff to keep us close to the Shepherd. That's an awesome concept when you look at how God cares for us.

The use of The Rod and the Staff when we as prophets have various needs in our life. "Even though I walk through the valley of the shadow of death, I will fear no evil, for you are with me; your rod and your staff, they comfort me (Psalm 23:4)". Can you say assurance, prophet we have that, when you understand the Ministry of The Prophetic Staff? This is a special ministry, unlike any other.

John W. Ritenbaugh[7] states in the Forerunner Commentary about the three ways the prophetic staff is used. It is critical to understand that the staff is used in three ways. The first is drawing sheep together into an intimate relationship, the shepherd will make sure the right lamb gets with the right ewe. To say this is critical is an understatement. There can be no hint of any confusion at all between the lamb and the ewe, the staff is used to hook the lamb around the neck through the body. The lamb is picked up and carried to another ewe. The is the second use, to pick the animal up with our hands. The smell of a human hands will give off the wrong odor, for mating. The staff, then, is used to bring the lamb into an intimate relationship with its ewe. This is the third use as the guiding into the right relationships is crucial. Sounds like us in our interaction among prophets and the general Body of Christ.

This is so true of us as we as the prophets of God use our staff to walk into an intimate relationship with God. We see the Spirit of God in the execution of the staff. We see gentle guidance whereas the rod suggests sterner measures such as an offense or defense protection.

God will lead, and guides, by His Spirit. Jesus told His disciples that He would not leave them to fend for themselves, but He would provide another guide: The guide was the Spirit of truth, the spirit that will guide you and I into all truths. The ministry of the rod or staff is real.

Take the time to develop the Prophetic mentality needed to carry and minister with a staff if this is where God is calling you. Those of you who read this and are curious, I pray you are refreshed with the new revelation and you see God like you never have. Whatever your reasons for reading this, let me say, welcome to the prophetic ministry of the Prophetic Staff.

CHAPTER TWO

The Ministry Of The Prophetic Staff

THE ROD OF GOD

The "rod of iron" or the rod of discipline in the bible the rod has symbolized power and authority and yes destructive power as we shared in the introduction the word rod and staff can apply to one and the same thing. The disciples used rods, or staffs, to assist them as they journeyed from place to place. Jesus, as he sent the disciples out told them in Mark 6:8 to take nothing for their journey, save a staff only, no scrip, no bread, no money in their purse.[8] Do you find that interesting? This was really a critical part of ministry. This is still important today as well.

So now that you have been called to Prophetic Staff ministry, it is your staff, or rod, of the Lord is indeed strong a firm foundation. It will carry us over the most difficult obstacles of our lives.[8] I say our lives because our lives are the ministries we have been given. Get this, as we build the mentality of this anointing. The staff or rod is there through our most severe trials. We must learn this ministry and what it does for us so we will appreciate it.

All of us have learned the 23rd Psalm, let's go back, the rod or staff will illustrate God's tender and loving care, protection, guidance, and comfort over all of his people, particularly all those who are dwelling in the "house of the Lord." [8]Prophet embrace this fully right now.

The "rod of Moses," the "rod of Aaron," the "rod of Levi," and most significantly, the rod of Moses is commonly called the Rod of God, play such an important role in the delivery of Israel from Egyptian bondage.[8] This was the same shepherd's rod which Moses used in tending the flocks of Jethro, his father-in-law, in Midian.[8] Moses is in the wilderness and goes forth with his staff and we complain today when we are not around bright lights and big city. We seem so not to understand the process.

The prophet Moses on the back side of Mount Horeb, the Lord appeared unto him in a flame of fire and spoke to him out of a burning bush. You simply have to imagine how hard Moses may have held his rod, in fear. God says, "I have surely seen the affliction of my people which are in Egypt, and have heard their cry, Moses, I will send thee unto Pharaoh, that thou mayest bring forth my people the children of Israel out of Egypt (Exodus. 3:7,10)."

There must be a strange feeling Moses experiences and I'm sure he probably did feel inadequate to this great task. Many of us would have questioned God in his choice. Look at Moses as he says that, they will not believe me, nor hearken unto my voice: for they will say, The Lord hath not appeared unto thee.[8] Does this sound like something you may have been through, I have and I'm sure you may of you felt the same way also? Moses is like many of us, caught in our feelings and emotions and leaning on them in a critical time in our life.

God proves something to Moses on that day as he said unto him, what is that in thine hand? And he said, A rod. And he said, Cast or throw it on the ground. And he threw it on the ground, and it became a serpent; and Moses fled from before it (Exodus. 4:1-4). Imagine being called as you run away as Moses did, he hears God call him again.

He stops and returns, and God said unto Moses, put forth thine hand, and take it by the tail. And he put forth his hand, and caught it, and it became a rod in his hand.[8] This must be mind blowing to say the least. Are you at this place mentality yet for a supernatural miracle?

The great thing is that Moses like many of us, needed a faith builder. We the Prophets of God, in this generation are like our prophetic forefathers, we have our faith built by our afflictions and life drama and we see that God proves himself in our lives daily. Prophets, God is still asking each one of us this same question, What is in our hands? What will it take to make you believe that I'm your God the source of the supernatural?

Prophets, yes, we have the talents, the abilities, and even if we have material possessions, with a limited knowledge of the Truth, please remember this. All things, that God has put in our hands have been sanctified with the 'rod' of God's authority through the begetting of the Holy Spirit.

This is a life changing principle and we need to embrace. This is something I highly encourage you to never forget. Yes, it is life changing and supernatural. We may feel inadequate at times, and so unworthy of this honor, just as the great Moses did. We know that in our own selves we come far short of his glory, but this worked for Moses and will work for you and me. Let us begin today to embrace it, right now!

Exodus 4:11,12 should bring us prophets comfort. These scriptures state "The Lord said unto him, who hath made man's mouth? Or who make the dumb, or deaf, or the seeing, or the blind? Have not I the Lord? Now therefore go, and I will be with thy mouth, and teach thee what thou shalt say." Are you starting to see that it was the Rod of God?

This was the proof that Moses need to go forth and not doubt and feel unworthy. What has happened to you that made you realize this concept? What has happened that made you know God really was for real? In my rewriting of this book I discovered this in a whole new way.

Let's look at Exodus 4:17 which says, "And thou shalt take this rod in thine hand, wherewith thou shalt do signs." Look at Moses representing God, and Aaron the 'Word' of God. That's the weight of Glory upon him. God was particular as he pointed out the fact that this rod had been sanctified for use by, his prophets. Do you see the signs related to the deliverance of the children of Israel from Egypt? Do you see the signs today related to our deliverance from This unstable world through Gods prophets?

Again, did you notice that your Staff has to be sanctified? That is why everybody can't touch them or use them or handle them. Your prophetic staff or Rod of God or mine. They are not toys! This is so critical that you understand this once your staff is sanctified or offered unto God for his use.

You cannot allow your kids or anyone who does not know you or your ministry to walk with you or to play with your staff after it has been offered to God. It is holy and any armor bearer or anyone who walks with you, should have proven him or herself before they handle your staff.

The Staff will be sanctified to handle the warfare you will inherit as a prophet. How can someone handle your warfare and they can't handle their personal issues? This is critical, and yes, I have seen people who were not authorized to carry or handle someone's staff become affected by this.

The shepherd's rod has become the "rod of God" and Moses was to use this rod and perform certain signs before Pharaoh. Imagine God using you in this way. This is when you have gotten a deposited experience. God tells Moses, "When thou goest to return into Egypt, see that thou do all those wonders before Pharaoh, which I have put in thine hand, here again, we see the influence of the Rod of God, but I will harden his heart, that he shall not let the people go (Exodus 4:21)."

Yes, there is an anointing was on the staff of Moses, it was part of his mantle or his gifting. The same is true for you, and today there has to be an anointing on the staff to protect, inform guard, and deliver all in the name of Jesus.

I love the way God set this up. Think about this, the primary purpose of these signs was to convince the children of Israel that Moses was appointed by the Lord to be their deliverer.[8] In Exodus 4:5 where it says that Moses would perform these signs, "that they may believe that the Lord God of their fathers" had sent Moses unto them. This is clear and powerful.

Our awesome God is now exercising of his rod of supervision in world affairs and yes even today. We see prophecies being fulfilled on an almost daily basis, and yes many of us still struggle to see this, but as we grow we see many signs, and believe that the kingdom is very near. Matthew 24 spoke of the signs of his presence and his kingdom. What's awesome is that the people believed, and they bowed their heads and worshiped.

We must realize this is the supernatural power of God. Imagine the time is soon coming, however, when the rod of the Lord will utterly 'swallow up' the rods of authority of this present evil world, all of which receive their power from Satan, "the god of this world (2 Cor. 4:4)[8]". The question is will you or I be one of the prophets chosen to use our prophetic staff or Rod of God to illustrate the awesome power of God.

Looking at Revelation 2:27, the Lord spoke of the "rod of iron" that would be used to bring about the destruction of this present evil order of things, this we should look forward to. We must adopt the supernatural mentality and mindset. Look at how the overthrow of Satan was shown in the ten plagues of Egypt which were accomplished by the stretching forth of the hand of Moses with the rod of God. The issue here is that Moses had to know that God was with him and God would perform the needed miracle. This is a supernatural concept. This is a special mentality. This is what you will need to walk with a prophetic staff. The haters and critics of this generation will eat you for lunch if you do not have it.

OK, now let's look at Pharaoh no sooner had he let the people go he has a change of heart again and sent his armies in pursuit. His actions were despicable. Exodus 14 describes, about 3 million people, with the Red Sea blocking their escape and Pharaoh's army about to overtake them. Supernatural power was needed to overcome these odds. Let's be real here, once again the people complained to and against Moses.

What a scene this has to be, Moses said unto the people, "Fear ye not, stand still, and see the salvation of the Lord, which he will show to you today: for the Egyptians whom ye have seen today, you shall see them again no more forever. The Lord shall fight for you, and ye shall hold your peace (Exodus 14:13-14)." This was the word of God to his prophet.

Exodus14:13-16 tests the faith of Moses and the people for sure. Look as the Lord said unto Moses, "Wherefore crest thou unto me: speak unto the children of Israel, that they go forward: But lift thou up thy rod, and stretch out thine hand over the sea, and divide it: and the children of Israel shall go on dry ground through the midst of the sea (Exodus 14:15-16)." The Prophetic Staff, the Rod of God, at work, the element of the Supernatural power of God at work in the life of his prophet and the people whom he was sent to.

Prophets there will always be times in your lives when you will have severe trials and testings along this line. Rejoice this is our promotion and elevation time, can you believe in the supernatural power of God as Satan tries pursuing and destroying you, but God is there to intervene.

When the world and its distractions, cares, and problems seem to press in about us, prophets we can't become fearful and discouraged. Moses said to the children of Israel, "Fear ye not, stand still, and see the salvation of the Lord (Exodus 14:13)." He also said, "The Lord shall fight for you and ye shall hold your peace (Exodus 14:14)." The Lord will never leave nor forsake us,

The Prophetic Staff

and he will be "a very present help in trouble" (Psalms. 46:1). We have got to hold on to this.

I would have loved to have been there as, Moses lifted up the rod and stretched out his hand over the sea and the waters were divided and the people passed over. The image had to have been overweening for the people to see.

This is how the rod of God's Spirit and power overruling in our lives will indeed also bring about our deliverance from every trial we have and as prophets, we have plenty. We must remember that "There hath no temptation taken you but such as is common to man: our God is always faithful. He is who will not suffer you to be tempted above that ye are able; but will with the temptation also make a way for us to escape, that ye may be able to bear it (I Cor. 10:13)."

Moses and the children of Israel have crossed over the Red Sea and as they approach Mount Horeb. The Israelite s had grown very rebellious against Moses because of the hardships they were faced with, in particular the shortage of water to drink. This sure sounds like today's prophets and how they handle things.

Moses asks God, "What shall I do unto this people (Exodus 17:4)?" The people he speaks of need water and they are again crying out to Moses. Moses is somewhat fearful they he will be stoned. God speaks to Moses, go on before them, and take thy rod, the same one he held up for a miracle in the Red sea.

God tells him to smite the rock, and there shall come water out of it, that the people may drink. And Moses did this as all the people watched in the sight of the elders of Israel (Exodus 17:4-7).

One thing for sure, the prophet will see test after test in his or her life. Let's examine Exodus 17. As a heathen king who sought to make war with Israel, Moses said unto Joshua, choose us our men, and go out, fight with Amalek, who was fighting with Israel (verse 9). Picture Moses telling Joshua that he will stand on the top of the hill with the rod of God in mine hand (verse 9).

Joshua did what he was told by Moses and fought with Amalek. Now, Moses, Aaron, and Hur went up to the top of the hill (verse 10). When Moses held up his hand, that Israel prevailed: and when he let down his hand, Amalek prevailed (verse 11). This is the warfare position, I will share on later. Moses' being a natural man got tired, his hands were heavy; and they took a stone and put it under him. Moses sat, but he had Aaron and Hur to keep his hands up (verse 11). In other words, one on each side. The hands of Moses were steady until the going down of the sun. The miracle position of warfare allowed Joshua to discomfited Amalek and his people with the edge of the sword (verse 13).

Prophet, yes, the warfare is indeed difficult. The weapons of our warfare are not carnal but the pulling down of strongholds (2 Corinthians 10:4). Today our success in battle depends upon our faithful use of the "sword of the Spirit" holding it high, always having the banner of the word of Truth before us. This is a type of prophetic staff or rod of God.

Those who God will appoint to use the Prophetic Staff must practice this concept daily and can't afford to allow it to drag the ground. We will surely lose the battle if we do. Each one of us has an individual battleground of our flesh, daily it has to be brought into subjection. Prophet, the rod of the Lord, his word is as our weapon against the flesh and its weaknesses. Let us hold the rod of truth high and use it properly in our lives. Understand that this is one of the things that separated Moses from many other prophets. Moses even with his speech problem was articulate to know Gods word and Gods will and Gods intentions. This is why his staff, The Rod of God was an instrument of the Supernatural.

The Aaron and Hur anointing is needed so much today, we all need the privilege of "holding up the hands" of those more active in the ministry. We think it belittles us and we do so much to make one's feel bad and insecure and we don't develop and stifle them as they try to develop. We need to learn that prayer, temporal support, and particularly in the many little ways that may be opened to us to encourage others in the Lord's vineyard and elevate our profile on the battlefield for the Lord.

We need and must understand as we look to develop The Aaron and Hur Anointing as the foundations of our mantles. We then start to develop into the Moses type prophet of today and move in the supernatural power as Moses did.

Prophet sometimes a word of encouragement, of thanks, an expression of love and appreciation could be far more important than you may realize. We have to continue to hold up the rod of Truth even unto the going down of the sun.

CHAPTER THREE

The Ministry Of The Prophetic Staff

THE PROPHETS STAFF A PIECE OF WOOD

How could a simple piece of wood do so much? Let's explore this in Exodus 15:22-27. Moses, leads the Israelites into the desert, three days they do not have water and can't find it either. This is a real life-threatening situation. Imagine after some time they finally came to some water, and they are saddened the bitterness of the water. Bible scholar Steve Rodeheaver states the following:

"The water is simply undrinkable. The Israelites named the place "Marah", which means "bitterness." Imagine literally dying of thirst, finding water, then discovering that it was salt water. Not a good life or death."

I can imagine they were upset. There is a common theme of the Israelites being bitter as they grumbled against Moses seemly yet again. Moses cries out to God. God now shows Moses a piece of wood which Moses promptly threw into the water, the water was made sweet and the Israelites were able to drink it. Moses is a hero again. And now he leads them to a place called Elim which had twelve springs and seventy palm trees.[9]

Death is threatening, and we are constantly under attack like Moses. We see that Moses cried out to God and God made the bitter water sweet. This is a real clear message. Whatever and whenever we as prophets have bitter obstacles as we encounter in life's journey we can count on God to transform them, for our use. We should learn the lesson even if the Israelites did not. Right now, say "God lead me to my Elim".

God "showing" or "directing" Moses to a piece of wood means he was how to use the piece of wood. Showing or directing are root verbs of the word "Torah". Torah means instruction, it specifically refers to the class God gave Moses on Mount Sinai for how the Israelite's were to live in covenant with him who brought them up out of Egypt.[9]

Let's look at this, when Moses cast this torah tree into the bitter water, the water became sweet, so the people could drink. The Torah was for the people not for water. Let's go deeper, the waters of Marah revealed the bitterness that lodged in the hearts of the Israelites yet need I say again.

They constantly grumbled against Moses while Moses cried out to God. Here we see the external obstacle revealed the internal realities of their hearts. Every prophet needs to look at this over and over, Moses trusted God. The Israelites, constantly betrayed and displayed a lack of trust as they grumble amongst themselves and against Moses. This should remind some of you prophetic leaders and Prophets sent to the nations of what is so evident in the face of trouble are some of the same basic issues we deal with today. We must have and we all need deliverance from more than just Pharaoh, or any other leader.

We are sent to people who need deliverance from their grumbling, mumbling, bitter selves. Therefore, our mentality must be in order. God teaches Moses about a piece of wood and the power of trusting him is the will of transformation.

How did Moses get his deliverance? The wooden staff, the piece of wood appeared in different forms depending upon the context. Moses' had an encounter with God, he saw a snake. Snakes are creatures of evil power and most fear snakes. We clearly see Moses did. Moses left the encounter knowing that God is all-powerful and can change a supportive staff to an evil force at will and the reverse. That is a simply fantastic concept.

Do you see, that before you can carry a staff, you must walk in a level of maturity that will probably be unmatched by many around you. You will see the issues you had to deal with, within yourself. You will then be able to deal with others as you have a deposited experience.

Notice that God tested the people after he uses Moses to sweeten the water with the piece of wood. We like Moses, needs to realize that the piece of Wood is a tool of God, as the Rod of God. In our hands it's a piece of wood, in his hands it's a tool of redemption.

Moses and Aaron each one of them carried a "staff or rod". A simply piece of wood, with maybe a small curve at the top. A piece of wood from the hand of Prophet Moses, who held the rod to perform miracles, to the High Priest Aaron, his prophet whose rod performed miracles without being held, the rod symbolized Gods Holy Hand. All this with a simple piece of wood.

The Israelites, observed the staff that brought forth miracles and wonders. We today need to do this as well. The Israelites also learned the staff's defensive capabilities in times of dangers. Again, this is not just a piece of wood but God's supreme power through the visual formation of wood.

Th is the rudimentary symbolization of the Hand of God being upon His people who chose to obey His Holy Will. This is demonstrated through the same piece of wood. We need the divine power of God, for the ability to see the supernatural power of God. The reality is that the staff was merely a functional piece of wood used by shepherds to guide their sheep or nomads to support the fatigue of the constant journey. Remember they did not have cars or dirt bikes, they walked.

There is no mystical connotation to the staff or rod. Both terms (rod or staff) are used metaphorically throughout the scriptures alluding to the Divine omnipotence of the Lord. Isaiah 10:5 says, "Woe to Assyria, the rod of My anger and the staff in whose hand is My indignation." Zechariah 11:10 says, "And I took my staff, even Beauty, and cut it asunder, that I might break my covenant which I had made with all the people." Zechariah 11:14 says, "Then I cut asunder mine other staff, even Bands, that I might break the brotherhood between Judah and Israel." Both of these scriptures proclaims the staff of strength denotes power from good and the staff of beauty denotes power from truth.

David, himself describes the use of the "rod and staff" most eloquently and beautifully in the 23rd Psalm. "Yea, though I walk through the valley of the shadow of death, I will fear no evil; for You are with me; Your rod and Your staff, they comfort me (Psalm 23:4)." Your rod and Your staff" denote the Gods Divine truth and good, which have strength beyond measure for anything that we will ever have to deal with. Thank God for assurance. Oh my, and I'm still talking about a piece of wood.

The rod or staff, still a piece of wood was referred to when kings designed their scepters. The terms are continued today by shepherds as their only equipment to guide and discipline their flocks in various countries. The rod made of wood, made of simplicity, once cut is without life. The Divine Glory of God's presence working through it gives it life, a different type of reality. That is what should excite you to know what was dead is alive with God. You want the supernatural? You got it prophet.

Guess what? we could look at the wood of the Holy Cross inspired with the Divinity of Jesus as he hung upon it. "The rod of Moses, the piece of wood with which he subdued the Egyptians, yes, it is the symbol of the cross of Jesus, who conquered the world." Somebody should be shouting about right now.

Jewish Scholoars, J. Frederic McCurdy and Louis Ginzberg states the following about Aaron's rod:

"A rod, a piece of wood, in the hands of Aaron, the high priest, was endowed with miraculous power during the plagues. Aaron's Rod swallowed the rods of the Egyptian magicians, and the same piece of wood blossomed and bore fruit in the Tabernacle, as an evidence of the exclusive right to the priesthood of the tribe of Levi. I am still talking about a piece of wood. When the Rod of Aaron produced blossoms, the Israelites could not but acknowledge the significance of it."

They could not ignore that God had chosen Aaron to administer the ecclesiastical affairs of the people as their High Priest There is a lesson here that applies to prophets. If we are using the rod of the Lord properly as prophets it will bring forth fruit unto the glory of God. Most of us as prophets today seem to expect to do great things all at once. We must understand that we go as far as our prophetic development is concerned. The concept is represented in the bud as we look at the staff of Aaron.

The bud is quenched, pinched off and not permitted to go on to blossom and fruition, many times, but God is not in a hurry. God patiently works with each one of us, giving us experiences that are best calculated to provide fertile ground for bringing forth these little buds for a long time.

We finally start to grow in the new Christ-like character called a prophet and our season to blossom out in great beauty is seen by others. Welcome to your process and know how to handle it. Can you say mentorship?

Do you want the Aaron's anointing? A call to be a prophet to a prophet called to a nation? Please understand that there will be a piece of wood spirituality in your life that will have buds, it will have blossoms, and will bring fruit all at the same time. All this from a piece of wood? Yes, all this from a piece of wood.

Remember this development will not be of your own ability, our own might or power, but only because of the spirit upon the rod. This is the spirit that dwells within us. Zechariah 4:6 says, "Not by might, nor by power, but by my spirit, saith the Lord of hosts."

CHAPTER FOUR

The Ministry Of The Prophetic Staff

THE POSITIONS OF THE STAFF

Prophet, understand that your staff is simply a dead piece of wood It has no life, none nor will it sustain any type of life. Once you surrender your staff to God, through your relationship, it becomes a tool of God. The Spirit of God gives It life, but only through surrender. Your staff is a tool of God to show miracles, signs and wonders. Your staff and my staffs are the proving vehicle to you that God is with you and will use you as Moses or any biblical prophet was used. Let's talk and deal now with the positions of the staff that God instructed his servants to use to facilitate signs and wonders.

POSITION OF PEACE

Exodus 14: 10-14 describes the position of peace. The sheer fright that the children of Israel were in when they perceived that Pharaoh pursued them, this was a highly emotional time. They knew all to well of his strength. They felt lost and his rage was evident. Picture this, they are on foot, unarmed, undisciplined, disquieted by long servitude, and now penned up by the situation of their camp, so that they could not make their escape.[10] This is not a good feeling to have or experience.

They had seen Gods power, and regardless of how disgusted they were with Moses, they cry out to him and still their fear set them a murmuring. Makes one wonder, from their perspective, where was God? Was God now not as able to work miracles The level of this being inexcusable was beyond disrespect.

The mega ingratitude to Moses, had been the faithful instrument of their deliverance and now the pressure upon them again. Oh, wow here come the emotions again as well. This is what the prophet of today must understand about people. Moses Instead of chiding them, he comforts them, and with an admirable presence and composure of mind.[11] Learn this today prophets it is our duty today that, when we cannot get out of our troubles, move our mind above our fears, this is called Prophetic Economy. The solution is always greater than the problem. Think that way. Moses did, but they had to learn this simple fact.

Moses assures them that God would deliver them. He told them that the Lord shall fight for you. Moses was confident and encouraged them also to be that way. This is a lesson we all need to learn as prophets during the storm of life.

Prophets the lesson we can learn from the Exodus account can be powerful and life-changing. When a prophet will trust God to fight their battles, it enables us to circumvent what often accompanies conflict, panic, fear, and hopelessness (Exodus 14:11–12). This is what Moses faced and the children of Israel as well. Have you ever been there when you can see absolutely no way around a problem, just like the children of Israel had to deal with?

I doubt if they figured that the Red Sea was going to split down the middle, providing their way of escape. Prophets when we believe God's Word of 2 Chronicles 20:17, they learn that no battle is too formidable or monumental for God to handle (Joshua 1:5).

Here we go? Look now at Moses, who was in the walking or standing position, it is also the position of Peace during the storm. We hear and honor God's word and how he has spoken to us, and we have the assurance regardless if anyone else does. Welcome to peace during the storm, and can you imagine how they were looking at Moses, calm, cool and collected.

A MIRACLE POSITIONAL

Exodus 14 tells us that the Lord hardened the heart of Pharaoh king of Egypt, and he pursued the people of Israel while the people of Israel were going out defiantly. God will test us and look at this, the Egyptians pursued them, all Pharaoh's horses and chariots and his horsemen and his army, and overtook them encamped at the sea.

The army of Pharaoh is near, the people of Israel lifted their eyes, and behold, the Egyptians were marching after them, and they feared greatly. And the people of Israel cried and say Moses, "Is it because there are no graves in Egypt that you have taken us away to die in the wilderness (Exodus 14:11)? And Moses said to the people, "Fear not, stand firm, remember his is still in the position of peace here (Exodus 14:13). The salvation of the Lord, is always available for us if we will believe.

Have you ever feared rejection? Scared of something that made you feel worthless? Fear the most self-centered of all emotions. Fear generated by a perceived high degree of threat to what we believe is our well-being, and they felt fear big time! Prophet deal with fear as you believe what we have been instructed in, accepted, and practiced and that's God word and his will. This will eliminate what we perceive to be threatening us. Fear, no doubt is a powerful producer of conduct, for good or bad, depending upon who or what is feared and the direction of our response.

Psalm 111:10 and Psalms112:1 show us who we need to fear as we are positively directed toward the glorifying of God. When we are afraid of the wrong thing it can never produce good things for the prophet, it will always produce bad things.

Fear is everywhere. God spoke and said to Moses in Exodus 14:15-16 "Why do you cry to me? Tell the people of Israel to go forward. Lift your staff, this is a position for miracles and stretch out your hand over the sea and divide it, that the people of Israel may go through the sea on dry ground." Prophet shout Glory here! God says, "I will harden the hearts of the Egyptians so that they shall go in after them, and I will get glory over Pharaoh and all his host, his chariots, and his horsemen. And the Egyptians shall know that I am the Lord, when I have gotten glory over Pharaoh, and all his Army of chariots, and his horsemen (Exodus 14:17)."

In Exodus 14 we see how Moses stretched out his hand with his staff, over the sea, the position of Miracles and the Lord drove the sea back by a strong east wind all night and made the sea dry land, and the waters were divided. And the people of Israel went into the midst of the sea on dry ground, the waters being a wall to them on their right hand and on their left. The Egyptians pursued and went in after them into the midst of the sea, and when the word of God started to manifest, they said, Let us flee from before Israel, for the Lord fights for them.

There are other times we will see Moses pointing his staff toward heaven for needed Miracles and bring judgment and curses towards all who disobeyed God. Understand that God will deal with you differently than he may deal with another prophet and their staff. You may have to use your staff differently or in a different position. This is for Moses a position of miracles. I'm willing to follow the lead of Moses on this one.

A POSITION OF PROVISION

In EXODUS 17:1 there was no water to drink and the fall guy was Moses. Funny how they saw Moses, like many see Gods prophets today and are so distant and strange acting with us. They felt Moses wanted to kill them. Have you ever wondered why you are a prophet, sent to the Nations one day and a flop, failure, fraud in people's eyes the next day? Moses, the agent of God, has brought them salvation time after time, oh how soon we forget. However, when they are hurting, they lose faith. Therefore, we as prophets must be strong and understand the mentality of being a prophet and spend time in this area of prophetic study.

The Israelites traveled by stages for rest and refreshment. No one should doubt they needed a source of water at each resting place, people and livestock require significant amounts of water every day. Again, understand there is no water!

Look at these two scriptures. Exodus 15:23 which states, "At Marah, the water was bitter." This is a serious problem, a matter of life and death. Exodus 17:2 says, "The people gripped at Moses, and said, 'Give us water to drink.'" Remember I keep telling you Moses is the fall guy, as you will be when God sets you up to be used mighty. They complain about and to against Moses, demanding that he give them water to drink.

"Moses said to them, 'Why do you quarrel with me? Why do you test God (Exodus 17:2)?" Imagine Moses, telling them to trust God, is like many leaders telling someone hungry that they will get fed and they see no food. It does not communicate well, however, Moses makes it clear that their quarrel is not with him, but with God. Moses is God's servant and has been doing God's bidding. Exodus 17:3 says, "The people were thirsty for water there; and the people murmured against Moses, and said, 'Why have you brought us up out of Egypt, to kill us, our children, and our livestock with thirst?" This was critical for them, yes, they have seen God save them again and again from apparently hopeless situations. Funny how our flesh will override the providence of God.

Moses is routinely faced with a crisis after crisis. He always turns to God for relief. Richard Niell Donovan, bible commentator explains further:

"He asks what he should do because he fears that the people will stone him. Stoning is a method of execution by throwing stones at the guilty party. They feel Moses is the guilty party. This is a dangerous situation; our natural inclination is to fight or flee. God tells Moses to do neither. Moses is now instructed is to move to the front of the people to reaffirm his status as their prophet. He is again to take the staff which God gave him to use in miraculous ways."

Exodus 17:6 says, "Behold, I will stand before you there on the rock in Horeb." Moses is told to strike the rock with his staff. "You shall strike the rock, and water will come out of it, that the people may drink (Exodus 17:6)." Moses did so in the sight of the elders of Israel. God orders him to strike the rock, and Moses obeys. The elders serve as witnesses to the miracle. This was the time that Moses obeyed, exactly as God spoke to him. The simple position of striking the rock is self-explanatory. Welcome to the is the provision position.

THE WARFARE POSITION

In Exodus 17: 9-16, The first opposition of the children of Israel, while wandering in the desert was from the Amalekites, a group of nomadic raiders, as they attacked the children of Israel. Moses had Joshua led the troops into battle, Moses, along with Aaron and Hur, watched the battle from a nearby hill. Exodus 17:11, "So it came about when Moses held his hand up, the warfare position with his staff, we see that Israel prevailed, and when he let his hand down, Amalek prevailed." Eventually, Moses became tired, Aaron and Hur responded by holding up his arms in the warfare position. There was one on each side of Moses. By doing this, the Israelites were able to finally defeat the Amalekites. Moses' leadership is on display here as he is willing to accept the assistance of others.

Prophet even as we learn the position, we see a lesson the position teaches us. Oftentimes prophetic leaders like Moses find it downright difficult to trust others. We have our insecurities and doubts that we feel will compromise our integrity as leaders if we allow people to do certain things. We all have these tendencies, in our cultural ethic of self-reliance, loneliness and isolation that will ultimately handicap our effectiveness especially in prophetic ministry. To truly grow as prophets, we must, like Moses, be willing to embrace the support of trusted friends and advisers. Let us all take self-inventory. Columnist Daniel Gyebi further elaborates on leadership:

"Prophetic Leaders should consider good advice or help regardless of who offers it. Did you know that Jethro was not part of Moses' inner circus? He was not even among the people of Israel freed from slavery in Egypt, this man was a foreigner from another country. He clearly seemed to have a prophetic nature. Leaders should learn to embrace ideas and help from all legitimate sources, including sources outside their inner circles. Good advice often comes from those perceived to be outsiders many times they have a non-biased perspective. Jethro's advice was not asked for. He gave the advice in good faith."

It was obvious he watched how Moses handled his business. Jethro's concern, thank God was genuine. This today does not happen all the time. Prophets we don't know who God will send to help whether we solicit it or not. We should not ignore advice or refuse help simply because it was not solicited. This is a valuable lesson every prophet can learn to go through warfare of any type. It does not cost us anything to simply listen, we have discernment to accept it or deny it.

Give Moses credit, he recognized that he could not lead the war effort alone. That was why he appointed Joshua to lead the physical aspects of the war while he, Aaron, and Hur concentrated on the spiritual side. At the top of the hill, Moses with his staff in the warfare position was part of a team. Who is really on your team today as you take inventory of your life? Leaders who operate solo or listen to their own counsel are neither effective nor successful. Who are you listening to, whoever controls your ear controls your destiny?

Every prophetic leader needs an adviser and helpers who are versatile and can evaluate issues from many perspectives. This is the 360-degree perspective. Look and see all the possible angles and solutions that complement leaders' best qualities for the issues. There was unity, and everyone was in the right position. Notice that all these things had to be in place for God to move. Welcome to The Warfare position with your staff and all that comes with it. Let me be clear, God use you in warfare with your staff if you allow God to. This comes from your relationship with God.

CHAPTER FIVE

The Ministry Of The Prophetic Staff

THE PROPHET OF TODAY AND THE STAFF

In Mark 6:8 Jesus spoke to the disciples, and said take "no scrip, no bread, no money," only your staff. Prophets, we can take nothing of this world into the kingdom, but the proper use of the rod and staff of the Lord can and will get us there. The rod of God must go with us all the way into the kingdom.[8] We must become students of how we use our prophetic staffs.

Ezekiel is a prophet who reminds us of the role of prophet within the Biblical days, but also a role that is continued on today. John the Baptist was a prophet (Matthew 11:11). The disciples were called to be prophets. Most of us today have had to process the thought that I'm really called to be a prophet.

Some of us accept this better than others. This is a death sentence and we must accept that. The prophet that Ezekiel speaks about comparing the prophet to a watchman for Israel (Ezekiel 33:1-11), the cold bold reality is it has little or no relevance for us with our technology of today all over the world 24 hours a day all the time.

Bishop Thomas Gumbleton expodes on how we are called to be prophets and share the message of Jesus. He states the following:

"Ezekiel proclaims as he moves in to the role of the prophet: to speak for God on behalf of the people. And in Ezekiel's time, it would be like a watchman looking out for how evil might be creeping into the community, coming in not so noticeable ways, and the prophet speaks for God and alerts the community."

So today we have to understand that in your time, which is now, when we are given the assignment by God to carry a staff, it is like a watchman, because we are the watchmen of today. We are dealing with evil directly in front and around us, we see ourselves moving in a level of faith that none around you are comfortable with, simple because God has called you and not them for this task. This is the essence of what carrying a staff is all about. It is difficult for friends and family to imagine, accept and even process you're going through. Has God called you to carry a staff that's a question you must answer.

You've been incorporated into the body of Christ and identified for special service by your gifting. Our divine role as a prophet of God is to speak on behalf of God. This means that our faith must be elevated for the assignment that you have been trained for. The caring and ministering of and with a staff is relevant to who you are and your given assignment.

Ask yourself this important question now, how do I as a prophet go about resolving my feelings about carrying out the prophetic role that I have been given, in this case to carry a staff and to intercede on the behalf of God, to speak God's truth? How do I handle this?

So glad you asked the question. Look at Matthew 18:18. It describes a process that every prophet needs to be aware of. Matthew 18:18 says, "I will give you the keys of the kingdom of God. Whatever you bind on Earth will be kept bound in heaven. Whatever you unbind on Earth, heaven will keep unbound." Prophet you have the authority to resolve every problem. Your prophetic Staff, the piece of wood is your symbol of that very authority. This is the validation you need to know about when others tease, make rumors about you or try to make you feel like God has not called you to do this. Know God and know him through his word.

Look at what we see with Moses, Elijah, Elisha, Ezekiel and others do with their prophetic staffs. They binned and loosed what needed to be moved and Every prophet shares in this authoritative role to teach, to reconcile, and to be prophetic. Now can you relate to any of these prophets and their work. We all should have a biblical prophet that we relate to. This is your job to find out who you relate to, and study this prophetic mentor and you will learn much.

Living the prophetic life, paves for us to, have that unique role of demonstrating love for a brother or sister prophets through your prophetic family, that becomes a very powerful message of the love of Jesus. Most of us are still processing the development of our prophetic role, and we must get past this if we intend to grow. Some of you today will be maverick prophets simply because you do not want to submit or connect and grow with your peers. This is an ouch, no talk about a subject to a lot of prophets, especially those who have had a small measure of success that is seen and tangible. The reality is Moses would not have grown without Aaron and Aaron would not have grown without Moses. Can we fit your name in this equation? Can the same can be said for you?

I believe you're reading this book for a reason. You are hungry for the anointing, so go and search and find yourself. You can walk in the Mantle of Moses if you when charged by God go forth and do what God calls you to do.

Those prophets charged with the task of a staff must realize the staff is a support. The staff supports the hand and arm, and through them the whole body; wherefore a staff takes on the signification of the part which it immediately supports, that is, the hand and arm, by both of which in the Word is signified the power of truth. This is you prophet at your best. Let God use you prophet. You will have to spend time with your staff though in prayer and you develop and grow in God.

Some of you, may not think the staff is or was a big deal, look at the multiple meanings of the staff to different people, In Hosea 4:12 says, "My people interrogate their wood, and their staff will answer them; for the spirit of whoredom hath led them astray, interrogating wood means consulting evils." The staff answering means that falsity is thence, which has power from the evil which they confirm. The spirit of whoredom denotes a life of falsity from evil.

Psalms. 23:4 says, "Yea, though I walk through the valley of shadow of Death, I will fear not evil to me; for Thou art with me; Thy rod and Thy staff comfort me." Thy rod and Thy staff denote the Divine truth and good, which have power. Wow, see how it relates to others.

Today in this generation we see that the same signs that were being manifested to the pharaohs now to our leaders and kings, presidents, and dictators, and world leaders of the present time. Their reaction, though, is that of disbelief. Their hearts are hardened, and they refuse to believe that the Lord's hand is being manifest in the affairs of men.[8] God is and forever will be. Today's warfare is indeed difficult, and we know that the weapons of our warfare are not carnal. Prophet your success and my success in battle depends upon our faithful use of the "sword of the Spirit" holding it high, always having the banner of the word of Truth before us. As prophets we need to hold the rod of Truth high and use it properly in our lives.[8]

As a prophet understanding how to develop your staff Prophetic ministry will be critical. First, there is only the small beginning of progress represented in the bud. There are and will be times the bud will be pinched off and not permitted to go on to blossom and fruition. I know there is work for you to do, but God is not in a hurry in this until you're ready to go forth. Yes, no doubt your needed now but you're not going to be able to go forth now. Moses had to have some work done and even then, he was still a work in progress. We see a prophet do something wrong and we bury that prophet, and we forget we have done wrong ourselves. Oh yes there is still work to be done within each of us. God works patiently with each of his prophets. The experiences that are to provide that needed fertile ground for bringing forth these little buds, so they can blossom.

This is critical for a Prophet sent to the nations because it takes a long time, and then gradually this new Christ-like character begins to blossom out in great beauty so that it is seen by others.[8] This is a process that so many of us don't want to experience. We want to rush and don't think we need a birthing period, we want to go straight to the Nations or the people and there are no buds on our staff.

Prophets the development of Gods glory upon and in our lives, will not be because of our own ability, our own might or power, but only because the spirit that dwells with us. Zechariah 4:6 says, "Not by might, nor by power, but by my spirit, saith the Lord of hosts."

Even for a senior level prophet like Moses, knowing the Spirit of God is so important. Do you remember Numbers 20:7-13? Numbers 20:7-9 says, "God says to Moses, Take the rod, and gather thou the assembly together, thou, and Aaron thy brother, and speak ye unto the rock before their eyes; and it shall give forth his water, and thou shalt bring forth to them water out of the rock: so, thou shalt give the congregation and their beasts drink. And Moses took the rod from before the Lord, as he commanded him."

Moses, no doubt is frustrated and irritated. Dawn Bible Studies association quotes the following:

"He and Aaron gathered the congregation together before the rock, and he said unto them, hear now, ye rebels; must we fetch you water out of this rock? Can you tell Moses is irritated and simply mad at the people? And Moses lifted his hand, and with his rod he smote the rock twice: and the water came out abundantly, and the congregation drank, and their beasts as well. We still have a situation here with Moses. The Lord spoke unto Moses and Aaron, because ye believed me not, to sanctify me in the eyes of the children of Israel, therefore ye shall not bring this congregation into the land which I have given them. This is the water of Meribah; because the children of Israel strove with the Lord, and he was sanctified in them."

Can you see how special and important the staff was and is Staff is? The staff affected the life of Moses as well as Aaron, the staff will affect your life as well. This was the end of a ministry because of a lackluster attitude. We really need to check our attitudes.

Moses, being provoked by his anger to the people, smote the rock twice, rather than speaking to it as God had instructed, and water came out abundantly. Moses and Aaron tempted the Lord by striking the rock twice in disobedience, they were not permitted to lead the children of Israel into the land of Canaan.[8]

This is a very important lesson for us as prophets. We are the ones who need to have a special relationship with him and we are the prophets of God. We must be properly instructed in the word of God, and even in the very smallest matters as to our conduct and attitudes and our business. Everything matters.

Read it again. In Mark 6:8 Jesus says take "no scrip, no bread, no money," only your staff. Prophet, we simply can take nothing of this world into the kingdom, but as we learn the proper use of the rod and staff of the Lord can and will get us there. When I understood this revelation, I knew that anything was possible with the supernatural power of God. Today we can and will still operate in the Supernatural power of our God, we are his prophets.

CHAPTER SIX

The Ministry Of The Prophetic Staff

HOW DO I FIND MY PROPHETIC STAFF?

Let's look at this and understand this clearly. There is no prophet nowhere that can identify what they don't know or better yet choose not to know. We must constantly learn. Prophet if you don't know who you are, you can't identify your prophetic staff, even if you believe God has called you to have one.

To find your staff, you need to know and be sure as to who you are. This must be clear. The notes of previous lessons on the Prophetic Staff, should have awakened you to see the importance of knowing who you are. The process we saw with Moses as he spent 40 years in one place, events of his life changed his status and another 40 years in the wilderness and only after his life changing encounter with his staff did he realize who he was. Let this sink in and know what you need to know.

Exodus 4:2 says, "What is that in your hand, Moses?". God goes on to explains the importance of what is in the hand of Moses. You and I are like Moses as you find your staff, and once we find it, we must know how to prepare it for use today. Your staff like the staff of Moses, must become the Rod of God. This is not for debate. Moses' staff is no longer his staff, but it is the "Rod or staff of God."

I have discussed with you that the Staff was the object of power and freedom for the people of Egypt. This was how they knew God was with Moses.

The staff represented Moses' calling in life as a shepherd. You staff will represent your calling as a Prophet. This will be part of your prophetic calling card. God is saying to you and me, he will take our staffs and perform miracles through it". Moses' perspective changed clearly about the way he looked at his staff. This is what you and I will expect God to do for you as you become as one with your staff. You will see the change in yourself and the expectation of miracles to be performed through your staff. This is so awesome, and you must know and remember this is faith at another level. Welcome to trust, my brother or sister prophet. There is much to the song, I will trust in the Lord.

Can you say more than a staff? Os Hillman states, "When a shepherd received a staff, it was made to last a lifetime. The wood had a creosote-type substance added to it to insure its hardness, giving it a long life. Therefore, the staff of Moses was more than a simple shepherd's staff. That staff represented his work and his very life."

You staff and my staffs represent our work, our lives as Prophets of God. We have been called to carry prophetic staffs, yes today in this time. They are very personal. Sure, Moses kept sheep in line with his as well. The more important, fact you need to see is that, his very life. When you understand this, you will come into a new relationship and understanding of your staff. Your prophetic Staff equates to spiritual power, the likes of you may have never seen before.

God transformed Moses' view of his staff, it was viewed differently. Your view will be different as well. This was representative of power and authority from God. This is what you must get as you study and work with your staff. You must get this, understand this is not for debate either.

The staff in his hand of a prophet represents that prophets calling as a prophet of God. At the bidding of God, you must know that you're giving up of your life to the prophetic ministry will expose you to dangers and situations. Some you will not have ever seen before. Your will and desire to escape will be great as you go through stage after stage of learning and maturing.

In Genesis 3 the serpent had been the constant enemy of the seed of the woman, and represented the power of the wicked one, which had prevailed in Egypt. But at the bidding of God, Moses seized the serpent by the tail, and received his staff again as 'the rod of God,' with which was used along with the staff of Aaron to smote Egypt with great plagues.[15]

Do you think for one-minute Moses had seen that before? The answer is no. From this sign the people of Israel would necessarily perceive, that God had not only called Moses to be the leader of Israel, but had endowed him with the power to overcome the serpent-like cunning spirit and the might Egypt's evil. Moses had to pick up the snake by its tale, something we are told never to do and some of us would not even if God said so.[15]

This is what, I mean as I tell you the prophetic will change you. God has changed the view of Moses, can you accept this for yourself, changing your old views of things, will change you greatly. God was now Moses' protector. Prophet he is your protector too. You must not ever forget this.

God says He also has a staff. Isaiah 10:26 says, "The LORD Almighty will lash them with a whip, as when he struck down Midian at the rock of Oreb; and he will raise his staff, whose staff, his staff over the waters, as he did in Egypt." This blows my mind to imagine the magnitude of Gods personal staff. Ponder this for a moment.

Can you picture this in your mind? See the vision here, Moses as he lifts his staff under the command of God. Literally God is going to use us to raise our staffs and he will manifest in every one of us at the same time, just as he did with Moses. Can he trust us with trouble? That we won't run or doubt him during the storm. We can use the authority that we see demonstrated in the life of Moses' given to him by God. Question, what are you going to do?

Today, as God's prophet see your staff as an instrument of transformation. The people of God have seen their staffs as mere instruments for accessing finances in their roles as shepherds.[15] You're the prophet of God, so shout glory prophet, as God is letting us know through Moses and now through us that our staffs represent much more. They are instruments that he will use to transform the very cities of our nations into places of freedom and love.[15] This is what we must deal with. We clearly have work to do. Are you called to this work?

As long we offer up our staffs before the Lord and live right God will work through it. He works on our behalf. We can't afford to lower our staff, we will miss the emphasis of its importance, we lose the blessing of God. Prophet, we must constantly offer up our lives to God for his protection and blessing upon it. This should be old new, but the fact is it is still relevant to each of us.

We offer up our lives and then we see the proof as, Moses places staffs before God in the Tent of the Testimony. The very next day it was Aaron's staff, that had represented the house of Levi, sprouted but also had budded, blossomed and produced almonds. This is a sign that God will use a very personal item like our staffs to show his approval upon our life.

Os Hillman explains how Satan desires to steal your staff and your destiny.

"God will confirm the anointing and leadership of his leaders. We really learn a vital lesson about the importance and value of the staff in the story of Judah. Judah, one of the twelve sons of Jacob. Judah's son Er was married to Tamar. Er was a wicked man, which the Lord judged and killed. Understand the customs of the day and time, the custom was that the brother was to lie with the deceased brother's wife to insure the lineage would continue. Do not try this now! Onan, the brother, did lie with Tamar but spilled his seed on the ground, and lost his life because of God's judgment. We now have a situation as Tamar, has no relative to carry on the seed. Her father-in-law, Judah fails to make any provision for Tamar and tells her to remain a widow."

Tamar is now full of shame. Consider the customs of the day.

What is interesting is that Judah's wife has died, and he went through a period of mourning. After his mourning, Judah takes a trip to a town called Timnah. He takes a buddy with him and they decide to party as we would call it. Tamar hears this, and she poses as a prostitute simply to entice Judah. Tamar, who is in disguise has sex with him.

The payment for the sex was supposed to be a young goat (Gen 38:17-19). Judah did not have the goat with him, said he said he would bring it the next day. Tamar, asks for a pledge. The pledge was Judah's staff. His staff wouldn't you know had his seal. Remember this was who he was, his honor, his rank, his status. Understand the value of the staff. Judah signed over what represented his very life to the woman who now had the goods on Judah.

Judah hears through the grapevine that Tamar is pregnant, and he is the first to accuse her of prostitution. Wonder how he felt when, Tamar reveals the owner of the staff as the father of her child. Judah must confess and repent.

Prophet, Satan wants to steal your inheritance. He wants to destroy your calling. He systematically destroyed Judah, and he will do it for you and I. You may want to carry a staff, and if you do, understand the responsibility. Your destiny is more important than the games of Satan. You staff carries that much weight and you must understand how important and vital it is to you, or your ministry may be destroyed. That's real talk.

I needed to share all of what you just read to show you how series the Prophetic Staff ministry is. Now when you do go to find a staff, you will need to be in pray. Let me strongly suggest how to proceed. Sure, you could buy a staff from online, but there clearly is a lost of personal interaction with God.

So let's begin. Find a place that you feel good about, a wooded area, where you feel the Spirit of God. This is very important. This place must be a place where there are potential wood staffs at, remember that. Then search for an adequate piece of wood that you know you can handle. It needs to be at least as thick as your arm, but smaller than your thigh.

The length will vary depending on your leadership. This is critical to know. The rule of thumb your staff should be no longer than your leaders staff. Those of you who try to outdo your leaders will never get the staff or the anointing God wants you to have. This is a very sensitive ministry.

Your staff should max out in length at the middle of your neck if you're not sure. Some may be longer or shorter that will depend on the prophet. Your staff may have marks of significant events that you may not understand called numbs that you have cut off to make your staff a workable tool of your prophetic ministry. Every mark on the wood means something.

Prophets please understand that a good staff starts with a good piece of wood, of course. The size, shape, sturdiness, and age of the wood all contribute to the quality of a potential prophetic staff.[16] A good Prophetic staff usually starts as a fairly straight piece of wood, look for a piece of wood that you can trim and sand down.

Hardwoods like oak and redwood tend to make the most manageable and sturdiest staffs. There are other options include maple, alder, cherry, aspen, among others. Always look for fresh hardwood, avoid sticks with holes or other evidence of insect activity. The stick may be weakened by insect boring, or you may unwittingly transport bugs into our home.[16]

Now that you have identified your staff, cut the staff with some type of saw or ax . Once you have cut it to specs I mentioned, and now you are ready to skin it. The bark needs to be removed and sanded until the staff is smoothed. Use short, quick, shallow strokes. You don't want to dig into the wood. Good, safe whittling takes time. Do this until it is as smooth as your skin. You can use whatever you need to get the job done, such as a pocketknife, larger knife, to whittle away the bark.

Always make sure you use the whittling tool that is most comfortable for you. Always whittle away from your body, with your legs or any part of your body totally clear. Knots in the wood could cause the knife to jump and slice or puncture you. That would really hurt so safety is always a concern and never neglect it.

Continue to whittle until the bright wood beneath is exposed. Depending on the type wood, some trees have multiple layers of bark, so keep at it until you can see the wood grain. Let your stick dry out after this. Fresh wood is better for trimming and whittling, but dried wood provides more rigidity and durability. Drying time will depend upon a host of factors, including wood type, environmental conditions, and your personal preferences.[16]

Allow for 2 days up to 2 weeks as the average target time. This step is critical, to say the least. Finally, let the stick dry until it becomes rigid but not brittle. Wood that dries too quickly can become brittle, so if it is extremely dry indoors, you may want to let your stick cure in a covered outdoor location, like a garage or shed.[16]

Prophet be real sensitive to the conditions of your area and your wood type. This will define you, and will be your prophetic calling card for a high-level walk in the anointing. Now you are ready to paint and varnish it. Time and patience are your best friends in this whole process.

Tools you may or will need are a knife, ax, chisel, hammer and saw, gloves, sand paper of multiple grades. A leather lap apron is an option, but you may use whatever you are comfortable with. Again, your total safety is critical and needed as you go forth in putting together your staff. There may be a need for you to do more than one staff and I would strongly suggest that you be in prayer about that. I would also suggest that you master the elementary level of The Prophetic Staff Ministry before you take on another staff. This will be many of the things we have already discussed.

Once you have your staff, completed and prepared your staff now it needs to be offered to God. This will vary depending on your leadership. Our ministry has a specific way we do it as to follow the basic guidelines, I have shared with you in this book.

You should have a better understanding of David as he wrote the rod and staff comforted him. God warns us against depending on our own strength to live the Prophetic life, I wish I could pour this in to you. Do not blow this off. By now you should realize that Jesus modeled a life born out of weakness.[15] Let's put ourselves there prophets, a life born out of our weakness and not our strength. God works through weakness prophet, get this and you're going to soar with the Eagles of God.

When you and I, prophet, depend upon our limited strength, it becomes a splintered staff. We must totally stop this because a splintered staff creates a painful infliction. A splinter can cripple you if it is not removed, are you tired of being crippled? So too, now our staffs, when used through our own strength becomes a source of our pain. We have enough pain and we now must breakthrough.

This is supernatural breakthrough and you and I will witness this through our weakness, not our strength. Prophet, we all must learn how to walk with God in such a way as to receive from God out of your obedience, not our sweat and toil[15], this is the lesson we must learn. Even as you find your staff, there is a lesson within that, as you can plainly see.

So you say, Prophetic Staff Ministry is what you have been called to, well this is where you will see the activity of God in your life and work, it will be reflected in your staff. Prepare like you are serious, as this is serious.

CHAPTER SEVEN

The Ministry Of The Prophetic Staff

WHO CAN CARRY YOUR STAFF?

The topic of this chapter is who can carry your staff? Why would this be important? We need to start with Elijah. He becomes a mentor to Elisha. Every prophet should be familiar with this story, after meeting the Lord on Mount Horeb, Elijah leaves on assignment from God, to select a wealthy young farmer as the future prophet of the nation to one day replace him.

1Kings 19:19 says, "So he departed thence, and found Elisha the son of Shaphat, who was plowing with twelve yokes of oxen before him, and he with the twelfth: and Elijah passed by him, and cast his mantle upon him." What a sequence of events in this relationship follows as several years pass. The time finally comes for Elisha to be left to take the leadership that Elijah had held. 2Kings 2:1 says,"And it came to pass, when the LORD would take up Elijah into heaven by a whirlwind, that Elijah went with Elisha from Gilgal."

The story continues as Elijah was taken to heaven, Elisha now finds a prophet to mentor. His name is Gehazi and on the surface, all looked well, he faithfully served and did Elisha's bidding. He did if well if only for a season.

There was a Gentile Shunamite woman who had often given them lodgings as they traveled past her home. She was barren, and we see that, Elisha prophesied she would have a son. She had a son as well. The child dies, and the woman now lays the child on the bed used by Elisha and traveled to find the Prophet.

In 2 Kings 4:12 Gehazi was Elisha's "servant." He was in line for the double anointing that was on Elisha. Gehazi was a prophet-in-training who is afforded such an awesome opportunity. He is sent to respond to the desperation and distress of the Shunamite woman, who had her young son, tragically die. In 2 Kings 4:29, Elisha even gave Gehazi his staff the same staff that had been the instrument through which God worked his mighty deeds.

Watch this and consider this strongly Gehazi has appeared in a reasonably positive light, but there may have been hints of his downfall. Prophets your attitude is so important. We see that Gehazi is callous and insensitive when he attempted to deal with the desperate Shunamite woman.

Elisha has still though enough of Gehazi to put his staff in Gehazi's hands, and instructs him to go directly to the dead son, and to lay his staff on the child's face. The issue is that nothing happens. Where is the anointing that had been demonstrated through the staff?

Ok your Gehazi, how would you feel when you lay the staff on the face of the woman's son and nothing happens? Gehazi had seen Elisha perform several notable miracles, yet the power is not there for him to perform a miracle himself. Prophets this is past critical, and you must look at this and see this. Also look at the fact if Elisha gave him the staff, he had confidence in Gehazi that he could be a vessel of Glory needed for the miracle.

Gehazi was given the Prophet's staff, as a sign of authority, and commissioned to go straight to the dead boy and revive him.[17] While we may feel that several things may have happened on his way there, the reality is that nothing happened, as he placed the staff on the child. What is going on and why? The relationship with his leadership is out of line and his attitude and ability to follow directives must be questioned.

Elisha himself then goes to the house of the Shunamite and shut himself up with the dead child. He prays, God restores the child, this was a future prophet by the name of Habakkuk.

Questions remain, what happened with Gehazi? We need to understand this because what if you or I had been sent by a prophet to someone in dire distress and we were no help? We seem to constantly forget we are the spiritual specialists, the prophets. Elisha would not have sent Gehazi if he did not feel he could have handled the situation. The anointing was available, and answers are needed here, to understand the sensitivity of the Prophetic Staff Ministry.

The Staff of Elisha, like the Staff of Moses and other prophets was a symbol of the authority of God that was with him and working through him. Elisha sending his staff, was like he, himself to be there. The understatement is that this woman did not have faith in Gehazi and she wanted to see Elisha., whose faith shines out here as an audacious and a bold faith.

It is not a reach to say that Gehazi was Elisha' servant, who was out of touch with the Lord, and even though he had Elisha's staff in his hand. Gehazi was commissioned by Elisha when he laid the staff on the child nothing happened. What am I saying, I'm saying that Gehazi was a mere formalist?

.Gehazi like many of the prophets today who do things differently than the plan of God, have the form but no power (2 Timothy 3:5). Yes, this is an additional challenge to Elisha's faith.

The staff of Elisha, like Moses, had great power in it. God's anointing is not transferable to other prophets who are not of your spirit. Gehazi proved that. The staff did not work for Gehazi and he was close to Elisha, but he did not have the spirit of Elisha. Be careful of people who walk with you, they must prove themselves over time. People who walk with you and say they are sent by God and when they don't or can't catch your spirit, this is what happens.

Elisha's and his staff were inseparable. Like a prophet who God has put his stamp of approval on, you see his staff represented his life and the anointing received from God. Every prophet must go through his own personal circumcision of heart experience to receive God's anointing. We can look at two things here. Gehazi had not experienced this and there is a part of me that wonders did Elisha miss this fact? We have to consider as great as Elisha was, he could have missed this, he was still human like you and I. Every prophet will miss the mark sometimes. Remember we are talking about a sensitive topic in a sensitive ministry. We are still learning about the supernatural and we have not arrived as many would want other to think they have.

Gehazi clearly reminds us of many of today now generation prophets, who aspire to be great, but don't want or simply will not put in a great work ethic, they seem to labor in suspect character, and their motives hide in devious fashions of flattering words and open-ended promises and a rhetoric of prophetic utterances that have been recited for years. Welcome to the prophetic ministry that is common and easy to function it, but you don't want. You will not grow in this type of ministry.

Some of you who know this story my feel like Gehazi's inability to revive the Shunamite woman's dead son was through no fault of Elisha. There is merit to this because of his own actions. Gehazi was given very specific instructions that Gehazi not speak at all until he had gone to the child, placed his staff upon him, and revived him. Did he do this? What happened?

A total lack of focus? The reality is it does matter who walks with you. It would really make one think that Gehazi, may have made a joke out of the situation. Can you see him asking people "Do you believe this staff can resurrect a dead child."? The Gehazi type prophet will not do will in the prophetic much less the ministry of the prophetic staff.

The reality that was expected was that Gehazi would immediately use the staff to revive the child. This would have taken him to another level, faith wise. This again is faith at another level, there is no doubt. The uselessness of Elisha's staff in this context is significant.

Gehazi, is living and serving daily in the presence of a great prophet.18 He is constantly involved in his work and witnessing the anointing. Notice that it still does not, allow him to experience the same degree of success. Gehazi was ruined by familiarity[18] and his lost sense of appreciation for what he had.

There is no doubt he had followed Elisha with genuine admiration and had the purest of motives.[18] The spirit of familiarity little by little, was dulled and drained of its wonder by repetition and familiarity.[18]

Did Elisha not understand that your staff should always be sacred even in the day-to-day tasks should become sacred. This is part of the common task to find divine glory in everyday living.

Gehazi, is like many of our generation prophets, as we live so continuously and so carelessly in the presence of fine things that they lose their significance.[18] Therefore, we see that those who walk with you must have your spirit, if they are to carry or handle your staff. The reality is if you are suspect then you have an obligation to not allow them access to your prophetic staff.

The one who you allow to handle your staff must be as one with you. You will do yourself a great injustice if you allow someone who has not proven themselves to handle your staff because you may want a certain look or perception about your ministry. I would suggest that someone who handles your staff have been with you at least 5 years. They would have seen all phases of you by then and they are still there and still faithful to God.

When I say handle your staff, keep in mind that I mean handle your staff with their bare hands. This means it is out of the cover or protective cover which should be a hard-plastic protective covering, or a covering you can handle. That will vary from prophet to prophet.

CHAPTER EIGHT

A Closing Thought

This is a difficult ministry for some prophets. The ministry of a prophetic staff is clearly not for every prophet. There is no shame if you are not called to this ministry. The obstacles you will have to overcome to relevance will vary. There may be those who will doubt and mock you in various ways. Your being prepared for the multiple challenges will be the key to your supernatural intimacy with God.

May I strongly suggest you seek out someone to work with, who will empower you in the pursuit of your Prophetic Staff Ministry. Prophets empower each other when they are not jealous of each other. They know who and whose they are, and they understand that in order to reach their destiny, they must learn and practice empowerment. On a personal level, your ability to grow in the prophetic staff ministry is going to be equivalent to your relationship with God, your desire, your relationships and your ability to focus. This is the package you must have together to be effective.

The world we live in today sees differently than we do. They see with a different standard. This adds to why we, as prophets, are always seemly looked upon differently than other ministries. This is a unique ministry, and you may be called names and thought of as ungodly even by some of your peers. You must know what you need to know to carry the prophetic staff.

I pray you have been introduced and elevated in prophetic staff ministry by your reading of this book. My wife, Prophetess Sabina Cox and I have been using our staffs for years, and we continue to use them and grow in the Prophetic Staff ministries. Remember this: anything that God deems worthy of his Glory is something we want to continue to grow in.

I look forward to seeing you at the next meeting, and if God says so, we will use our prophetic staffs. God bless you in your growth in the Prophetic Staff ministry. Call our office at 919-695-3375 if we can assist you or email me at ApostleCox@gmail.com

Blessings

Apostle Ken Cox

Where Eagles Fly

ABOUT THE AUTHOR

Apostle Ken Cox started serving God in 1994 after a series of unforeseen life failures. Out of the military and seemly starting life over again, by 2000, Apostle Cox had found his life calling as a Prophet. The challenge of learning and understanding presented a new frontier. Apostle Cox dove into the process and has now emerged as a well-traveled prophet who serves the Body of Christ as an Apostle.

Apostle Cox, along with his wife, Prophetess Sabina Cox are the leaders of Where Eagles Fly Fellowship Inc., a fellowship of prophets and apostle across the USA and beyond who are dedicated and focused on establishing the prophetic gift back into society as they raise up prophets around the country and abroad.

Apostle Cox and Prophetess Cox are available for Revivals, Conferences and Meetings. They have been featured in meetings and sought-after to teach and instruct the prophetic for ministries seeking to learn more about the gift.

Apostle and Prophetess Cox have 3 children and 4 grandkids as of this writing and currently reside in Durham, NC. Contact them through the Where Eagles Fly office at 919-695-3375 or 919-213-1328 or at www.whereeaglesfly.us.

He is the author of The Following:

"The Prophet In The Wilderness"

REFERENCE

1) Matteh. NAS Exhaustive Concordance of the Bible with Hebrew-Aramaic and Greek Dictionaries Copyright © 1981, 1998 by The Lockman Foundation All rights reserved Lockman.org

2) Maqqel. H4731 - maqqel - Strong's Hebrew Lexicon (KJV). Retrieved from https://www.blueletterbible.org//lang/lexicon/lexicon.cfm?Strongs=h4731&t=kjv

3) Shebet. H7626 - shebet - Strong's Hebrew Lexicon (KJV). Retrieved from https://www.blueletterbible.org//lang/lexicon/lexicon.cfm?Strongs=h7626&t=kjv

4) Rhabdos. G4464 - rhabdos - Strong's Greek Lexicon (KJV). Retrieved from https://www.blueletterbible.org//lang/lexicon/lexicon.cfm?Strongs=g4464&t=kjv

5) Webster's Revised Unabridged Dictionary (1913)." Edited by Noah Porter D.D., LL.D., Webster's Online Dictionary - with Multilingual Thesaurus Translation, C. & G. Merriam Company, 22 Feb. 1998, www.websters-online-dictionary.org/credits/websters1913.html#

6) Wellman,. J. (2015, July 24) What Is The Difference Between The Rod and The Staff? A Bible Study Retrieved from http://www.patheos.com/blogs/christiancrier/2015/07/24/what-is-the-difference-between-the-rod-and-the-staff-a-bible-study/#sGLqZWqoAqswB0iG.99

7) Ritenbaugh, J.W. (1992) Shepherd's Staff Used for

Inspection. Retrieved from https://www.bibletools.org/index.cfm/fuseaction/Topical.show/RTD/cgg/ID/14587/Shepherds-Staff-Used-for-Inspection.htm

8) Dawn Bible Students Association (2009).The Rod and Staff of the Lord. Retrieved from http://dawnbible.com/2009/0908cl-2.htm

9) Rodeheaver, S. (2011, November 8). Exodus 15:22-27: Bitter Water and Sweet Wood. Retrieved from http://www.crivoice.org/biblestudy/exodus/bbex21.html.

10). McCurdy, J. F. and Ginzberg, L. Aaron's Rod (2002) Retrieved from http://jewishencyclopedia.com/articles/5-aaron-s-rod

11) Stepbible.(2018). Retrieved from https://www.stepbible.org/?q=version=MHC|reference=Exod.14

12) Donovan, R. N.Biblical (2010).Commentary Exodus 17:1-7 Retrieved from https://www.sermonwriter.com/biblical-commentary/exodus-171-7-commentary/

13) Gyebi, Daniel. (2014, January 29). When Leaders Need Help - The example of Moses. Retrieved from https://www.ghanaweb.com/GhanaHomePage/features/artikel.php?ID=299127.

14) Gumbleton, T. (2014, September 11). REFLECTION: Each of us is called to be a prophet and share Jesus' message. Retrieved from https://paxchristiusa.org/2014/09/11/reflection-each-of-us-is-called-to-be-a-prophet-and-share-jesus-message/

15) Hillman, O. (1996). The Power of the Staff. Retrieved from http://www.intheworkplace.com/apps/articles/default.asp?articleid=68279&columnid=1935

16) How to Make a Walking Stick Retrieved from https://www.wikihow.com/Make-a-Walking-Stick

17) Cole-Rous, J. (2010). Gehazi - A Powerless Prophet. Retrieved from http://globalchristiancenter.com/christian-living/lesser-known-bible-people/31275-gehazi-prophet-without-power

18) Williams, C. E. The Tragedy of Gehazi. Retrieved from http://www.ecclesia.org/truth/gehazi.html

GLOSSARY

Anoint (anointing)
- to put oil or ointment on, especially as part of a religious ritual that confers honor and sacredness.

Authority
- the right, power, or ability to give orders, make decisions, or demand or compel obedience.
- (usually plural) those who have this right or power by law
- force of execution; mastery.

Connotation
- a secondary meaning or implication of a word or expression, in addition to its primary meaning.

Deliverance
- the act or process of delivering.
- the state of being set free.

Destruction
- the state of being destroyed; ruin.

Discipline
- training of the body or mind according to rules or principles
- control or determination brought about by training; self-control
- punishment for the sake of training or correction

Ewe
- a full-grown female sheep

Faith
- belief, confidence, or trust.

Lamb
- a young sheep, especially one not weaned
- Jesus Christ

Pharaoh
- a king of ancient Egypt, or the title of any one of these kings.

Power
- the capability to act or function effectively.
- the ability to exert authority or control over others.
- a person, group, or nation that exercises authority or control, or that has wide influence.
-

Rod
- a straight, thin, usually round and inflexible stick, shaft, or bar

Sanctified
- made holy or sacred.

Shepherd
- a person who herds and watches over sheep at pasture.
- one who guides, protects, and oversees.

Staff
- a pole or rod often used as an aid in walking or hiking; walking stick.

Torah
- (sometimes capitalized) the entire body of Jewish law and commentary, both written and oral, especially the Old Testament and the Talmud.

INDEX

A

Aaron, 26, 41, 44

anointing, 51, 55, 60

B

battlefield, 19

bitterness, 21–22

Blessings, 65

blossom, 27, 43

C

children, 44

community, 39

congregation, 44

country, 36, 66

D

defense, 5

deliverance, 13, 70

discipline, 6–7, 9

E

Elijah, 57–58, 60–61

Elisha, 58, 62

Egypt, 11, 22, 47–49

escape, 30, 48

Ezekiel, 38–39

F

fear, 5, 7, 10, 25, 31–32

G

Gehazi, 59–61, 69

H

authority, 15

J

Jesus, 8, 14, 38–39, 41

Jethro, 36

Judah, 51

Judah, 51–52

L

leaders, 36, 51

Lord, 19, 26, 38, 44–45, 50–51

M

Micah, 7

Ministry, 9, 21, 28, 38, 46, 57

Moses, 3–5, 10–12, 17–18, 22–24, 32–36, 41, 44, 47–48, 68

P

power, 60, 70–71

powers, 27, 43, 70

prophetic staffs, 7, 13, 19, 38, 63, 65

prophets, 21–23, 26, 29, 31, 34, 36, 38–40, 42–43, 45, 48, 53–54, 58, 60, 63–64, 66

R

rhabdos, 67

rock, 44, 49

rod, 5–13, 19, 24, 26, 38, 44–45, 72

rod of truth, 19, 42

S

sheep, 7, 48

shepherds, 6, 24, 47

sovereignty, 6

strongholds, 18

supportive staff, 23

symbol, 6, 40, 60

T

tool, 24, 28, 55

truth, 4, 40–41

truth, 19–20, 42

W

warfare, 18, 36, 42

waters, 17, 21–22, 33, 44

wood, 21–22, 24, 28, 54

Z

Zechariah, 25, 27, 43

www.ingramcontent.com/pod-product-compliance
Lightning Source LLC
Chambersburg PA
CBHW071536080526
44588CB00011B/1692